MW01288595

5 POWERFUL MEDITATIONS TO HELP HEAL YOUR ANIMALS

Kathleen Prasad

Text, design and concept Copyright © 2015 Kathleen Prasad. All rights reserved. No part of this publication may be reproduced, stored in a retrieval system, or transmitted in any form or by any means without the prior written permission of the author, nor be otherwise circulated in any form of binding or cover other than that in which it is published and without a similar condition being imposed on the subsequent purchaser.

Publisher: Amazon
Production: Leah D'Ambrosio

DISCLAIMER: The suggestions in this book are not intended as a substitute for professional veterinary care. Meditation sessions are given for the purpose of stress reduction and relaxation to promote healing. Meditation is not a substitute for medical diagnosis and treatment. Meditation practitioners do not diagnose conditions nor do they prescribe, perform medical treatment, nor interfere with the treatment of a licensed medical professional. It is recommended that animals be taken to a licensed veterinarian or licensed health care professional for any ailment they have.

TABLE OF CONTENTS

INTRODUCTION

Meditation is a powerful doorway into a new paradigm of healing. It is a way for us to support our animals in the most gentle, yet powerful way possible. To be able to bring all our energy to this present moment with an open heart: this is the most profound gift of healing support we could ever offer another being. Meditation shows us the way to true healing through mindfulness, focus, grounding, expansion, and positivity.

When we meditate, we learn to shift our state of mind and begin to see with the heart. When we see with our hearts, we can remember the power of infinite healing possibility.

Meditation is about being mindful, but I believe you cannot be truly mindful without also being heartful—feeling and embracing the abundance of emotions and feelings in one's heart. Without the heart component, mindfulness leads to a calm and aware state of being, yes, but also to a state of indifference or detachment.

In Japanese, the character "kokoro" means mind and heart (the same). So in Japanese tradition, your mind has to unify with your heart for you to be in the "right" space for healing. This idea—a fusing of heart and mind—fits well with the idea of

1

meditating with animals. When we sit or walk mindfully with our animals, our hearts open so we can radiate our inner compassion. And with our animal companions by our side, offering their unconditional love and acceptance of us, we are able to access this same place within ourselves more easily. The heartful contemplation that follows, promotes generosity, openness to others, healing and most of all, compassion.

Too often, we underestimate our inner power and potential. We also might underestimate the power of compassion to help turn things around not only for us, but also for those in our life, for our animals, who desperately need healing.

When we sit in meditation with our animals, we must break free and transcend our difficulties—we must merge our state of mind with our heart. In so doing, we access our inner compassion, which can help our animals find peace. But how can we do this if we don't have peace within ourselves, or even more, if we've lost our faith that peace exists? When we look within, we are reminded that peace, compassion and love are all right there, just waiting for us. When we remember to look with our hearts, we will see it.

The benefits of meditating are well known, and the best part is it's even more fun with your animals. It can be done anywhere; meditation doesn't require a formal setup. You can do it while walking the dog, while in the pasture with your horse, while sitting still on a bench. There really is no wrong way to meditate, as long as your heartful intention is there.

Below are 23 ways meditation can improve your life right now. Invite your animals to share your meditation and make it even better!

1. **You'll sleep better.** Insomniacs, rejoice! Mindfulness meditation improves the quality of a person's sleep, especially in older adults.

2. **You'll lower your blood pressure.** Studies have indicated that mindfulness meditation, which helps you let go of pent-up tension, is a natural way to help lower your blood pressure. Some people even attribute their daily meditation discipline to allowing them the ability to reduce their dependence on blood-pressure medications.

3. **Meditation helps you to better handle stressful situations.** When you are able to get into a quiet, mindful space on a daily basis, you'll feel calmer overall, allowing you to regulate your emotions and better handle the daily stressors that typically might send you over the edge.

4. **Meditation decreases depression and anxiety.** Mark Ruffalo is one celebrity who has spoken out about how meditation "saved him" from

anxiety. Countless others with depression and anxious thoughts are feeling the benefits as well. Even cancer centers across the country offer meditation rooms for patients. Training our thoughts to focus on the "right now" instead of anxiety-producing thoughts is so helpful when you're going through a tough time. And yes, I know this from firsthand experience, too!

5. **Meditation helps to relieve pain.** Amazing but true: Studies have shown that meditation can sometimes take the place of narcotics for patients who suffer from chronic pain. Though not a cure, as pain sufferers will tell you, even a small bit of relief can be priceless. I found meditation absolutely essential to help me relieve the physical and emotional pain of breast cancer treatment.

6. **You'll boost your immune system.** In fact, a recent UCLA study found that HIV patients who practiced meditation were able to "slow down" the drop in their CD-4 cells (these are the immune cells that are attacked and destroyed by the virus).

7. **You'll feel the positive results of meditation in just minutes.** It's true! In study after study, it's shown that you'll feel the benefits of meditation in no time at all. And though every minute counts, if you want to feel the best results, shoot for at least 25 minutes a day for three

consecutive days, according to Carnegie Mellon University.

8. **Meditation makes a person more compassionate.** A study, conducted by psychological scientist David DeSteno of Northeastern University and his colleagues, shows this to be true. And as I have found in my work with animals, the compassion and kindness we feel after connecting with our inner self through meditation extends not just toward fellow humans, but to animals as well.

9. **The "little things" won't upset you the way they usually do.** Meditating helps you to focus on the big picture of what matters in this day; it trains your heart and mind toward living mindfully and in the now. As a result, you'll feel better able to peacefully navigate your day when small stressors crop up. For added inspiration, try this book: *The Big Book of Small Stuff: 100 of the Best Inspirations from Don't Sweat the Small Stuff.*

10. **People who meditate are happier.** Happiness is something we all strive for, isn't it? Meditation helps to take us there—in fact, studies show you're actually "rewiring your brain" for happiness. Science says there are seven habits we can practice for a happier life. Guess what? Meditation will nurture all of them!

11. Meditation helps to boost your memory and ability to focus and learn. Students who took part in "mindfulness training" did better on the GRE than those who did not. And remember, kids are never too young to learn how to meditate (and experience the positive effects of it!).

12. Your overall quality of life will improve. In addition to all of the scientifically backed health benefits of meditation, you'll begin to feel more fulfillment in your daily life.

13. You'll feel calmer throughout your day. When you're able to find your Zen, you can bring balance into your family and work life, and your day will run smoother.

14. You'll be more successful in work. Meditation is a success secret of CEOs and famous actors. Even corporations like Google and Apple encourage their employees to meditate—because it helps the bottom line. The top three reasons everyone at Google is meditating are emotional intelligence, focus and resilience.

15. It can help you to quit smoking and other addictive behaviors.

16. Meditation can reduce your risk of a heart attack. According to the American Heart Association, meditation helps you to reduce the amount of stress you feel in life—which can help you combat cardiovascular disease.

17. Some researchers believe meditation can even protect against Alzheimer's and Dementia.

18. Meditation can help you manage grief. When dealing with grief and loss, it can feel as if nothing will ever help. But when you meditate, you are training your mind away from the hurts of yesterday and the fears of tomorrow. I used meditation to manage my grief when my beloved dog Dakota passed away.

19. Meditation helps you deal with traumatic events in your past. Related to #18 above, veterans and those suffering from PTSD have found much help in meditation.

20. It will help you to be present and really live in this very moment. How many of us rush, rush, rush through each day? But then we wonder where the day went and wish we could slow down. Part of living a mindful life is living (and enjoying) the moment as we experience it. Meditation can help you to embrace more of these moments.

21. You'll attain a better understanding of your deepest self. Meditation can help you answer this question: What is the true purpose of your life? Additionally, meditation can help to strengthen your connection to your intuition.

22. Meditation can help you feel inspired in new ways. Need to do some brainstorming? Is there a problem that needs solving? Focusing your mind in meditation can help you see things in new and different ways.

23. It literally reshapes your brain. Who knew "reshaping" your brain could improve your life ... but it does! All of the positives listed above result from meditation's physiological effects on the brain itself.

In this book I will not only share five of my favorite meditations to help you help your animals, but I will also share the mind/heart shifts we need to make to transform any situation into a peaceful one. In shifting ourselves, we can support healing in the animals who share the space with us. Where there is peace, there is healing. Where there is compassion, there is healing. Where there is love, there is healing.

TIPS TO REMEMBER WHEN MEDITATING WITH ANIMALS

Animals appreciate being invited to share a meditation space with you; in other words, being allowed to choose how and whether or not to participate. To ensure your animal's willingness to share a healing meditation space with you, here are a few suggestions for success.

1. Begin by dedicating your meditation practice to your animal. Do this with your whole heart.

2. Keep your mind focused as much as possible on your meditation, rather than on your animal's problems or on trying to "fix" what is wrong.

3. Do not initiate hands-on contact; allow your animal to relax at a distance from you or come forward for physical contact as he/she chooses.

4. Make sure your physical movement, position, posture and gaze are gentle and non-dominant.

5. Release your thoughts like clouds floating in the sky. Allow worries, fears, expectations and judgments to arise naturally and then let them go. Simply return to the breath.

6. Sit with your animal in meditation for 30-60 minutes. This gives your animal time to fully relax into the space with you.

7. Allow your animal to move freely and even leave the space where you are as he/she wishes.

8. As you complete your meditation, thank your animal for his/her participation and connection.

9. Pay attention to any healing shifts or changes which you may notice after the meditation.

TRANSFORMATION 1: FROM STRESS AND WHAT'S WRONG TO RELAXATION AND EXPANSION

In order to support animals who are ill or suffering, we have to let go of our focus on the problems because this makes our awareness so narrow that it becomes very difficult to find the space and potential to heal. The more open and expansive our mind is, the more relaxed our thoughts become, and the more we get in touch with our inner healing potential. When we feel that potential inside ourselves, we can help remind the animal of his or her own inner healing power.

Dwell on the beauty of life. Watch the stars and see yourself running with them.
– Marcus Aurelius

When we meditate, first we relax our bodies and our breath. Slowly our minds follow. When our mind lets go of all our anger and worries, trying to "do" and "fix," then our mind can drop down into our heart. The healing power of the heart is truly infinite. The more stable we become in this peaceful heart space, the more we can radiate it out to others. This is such a gentle and subtle technique, but also so powerful. Animals are very tuned into this kind of heart/mind practice. By practicing just some simple meditative techniques, we can begin to see healing results almost immediately.

A few years ago, my retired horse Shawnee had fallen, and he was standing on three legs when I arrived to visit. Of course all of my focus was on his injuries—his swollen knee and unhappy expression. He was groaning in pain with every shift of his weight, and it hurt my heart to hear it. As I waited for the vet to arrive, I suddenly realized that worrying and fretting about what was happening was not going to help him. Certainly, it wasn't going to help me. So I chose to instead meditate.

I stood with him. I breathed. I turned my mental focus away from all the things that were wrong in that moment and focused instead inward to find my still point. After several minutes, Shawnee relaxed and became much calmer, licking, chewing and even yawning a few times. By the end of half an hour, he was putting weight on his leg, his eyes were much brighter and he even began to graze and look for treats in my pockets. He was feeling so much better.

The vet arrived shortly after that and after the exam, my vet determined he was going to be okay and just needed some time to recover. I took the time everyday to spend time in quiet meditation and stillness with him as he recovered. I could feel in my heart this time between us was helping both of us. Amazingly, he always seemed to walk a bit easier afterwards and I, for my own part, felt much less worried about him.

When we meditate, the healing space expands to include both of us, and it can help both of us. I can relax and this helps my animals relax. Animals will join us when we meditate. Meditation opens our hearts so that we can come together in a heart-to-heart connection. When we touch hearts, a beautiful expansion happens which makes everybody feel better physically, emotionally and spiritually.

PEACEFUL BREATHING WITH YOUR ANIMAL MEDITATION

Sit comfortably with your palms resting on your lap. Now close your eyes and take a nice deep, cleansing breath and let it out slowly. Breathe in through your nose, filling your body with beautiful healing light all the way down to your lower belly, below your belly button. On the out breath, imagine this light can expand out your skin, out into your aura and out into the universe. Continue to breathe in through your nose, filling your body with healing light and connecting to the lower belly, and on the out breath, expand this light out into the universe.

Continue this deep belly breath for a few minutes. With each breath in, feel your connection to your lower belly growing stronger and deeper, and with each breath out, feel yourself expanding wider and wider into the universe. Breathe in, connecting to your lower belly, and breathe out, expanding into the universe. Return your breath to normal and take a minute; just sit in that beautiful space of energy created with your breath. Energy is inside of you and all around you. Feel the easy flow, the balance and peace. Very gently, simply invite your animal to share this beautiful space with you. Return to the deep belly breath to help keep your mind focused.

TRANSFORMATION 2: FROM AGGRESSION TO CALM

It takes an incredible amount of strength to remain calm amidst a chaotic situation. Yet this is what you will be able to do if you create a strong meditation practice with animals. I like to call those of you who choose this path, "peaceful warriors." Animals will be drawn to your strength when they need healing.

"A man of calm is like a shady tree. People who need shelter come to it. – Toba Beta

Meditation practice can help you to stay calm no matter what problems the animals you work with may face. You can be a shady tree for that animal; that calm can radiate from you, so that animals will come to you for support.

One of the most dramatic healing transformations meditation can create is when you are meditating with an aggressive animal. When an aggressive animal allows himself to fully relax, he can open up to the possibility of peace within himself. It's there, but he's forgotten it. When he touches that peaceful place, because you have reminded him about it by holding it within yourself and radiating it, then healing can begin again; the animal has taken the first step on the road to becoming balanced.

If you're working with an aggressive animal, it's important first of all to acknowledge your own inner fear or worry. Take a look at what the animal's aggressive behavior touches in you. Not only in that moment, but it can also bring up older fears from your life or your past. It's important to acknowledge that. Then, as much as you're able to, just let it go. Visualize clouds floating by. See those fears as the clouds, and they're just floating by in the sky. Try not to hold on to them or attach to them, just acknowledge them and let them float away.

To meditate, find a place separate from the animal where you will be safe, close your eyes and go inward. Dedicate your meditation to support this animal for whatever he's open to receive or nothing at all. Just embrace the idea that this animal is perfect and empowered at this very moment.

It's also important to visualize the animal as peaceful, calm and steady. In other words, as already healed and in perfect balance. If you look with your eyes, this is not what you will see, so you have to look more deeply and see with your heart. Imagine you can look beneath all the layers of hurt, sadness and anger that the animal is showing on the outside. You can see the animal's pure, perfect light–his inner essence and spirit. Allow yourself to see that peaceful heart even if the animal has forgotten it. Remember inner peace–truly believe that it's there, because it is! Your own attitude of hope and possibility towards that animal can help turn him around.

I remember working with a very vicious dog at one of the shelters where I was volunteering, and he was going nuts in his kennel. There was froth flying everywhere, and he was snarling and lunging when he would see anything move. I sat down outside the kennel several feet away, facing away from the dog. I closed my eyes and went inward. I imagined this dog was peaceful. I knew it was there inside of him even if he had forgotten it, and I just modeled it to help remind him. It didn't matter how he was behaving, I was that calm and shady tree.

After about fifteen minutes, I opened one eye to peek and see what was going on. It was amazing: he had stopped pacing lunging and barking. He was standing still, leaning against the wall of the kennel. His head was down and bobbing up and down as he fell in and out of sleep. He was trying his hardest to resist the relaxation, but he couldn't, because in his deep and inner heart, he also longed for peace. Yes, even this aggressive animal longed for peace. It was only through meditation that I was able to reach him.

We need to remember when we are with these beings that have these very strong difficulties they're facing, that they long for balance and harmony. Their hearts long for peace. If you can be that strong and peaceful warrior, or calm, shady tree, you can see amazing transformations.

To help you nurture peace in your own life so that you can share it more easily with animals, try these tips:

1. **Set your alarm 20 minutes earlier.** It's amazing how a change so small can accomplish so much. When you're not rushing to get out the door, you can take a few extra minutes for yourself. Read a few pages of the book at your bedside, sip your coffee, meditate, or snuggle with your cat. It doesn't matter what you're doing, just as long as you're taking a few peaceful moments for yourself. Starting each day with a few minutes of quiet time will help you tackle the rest of what's ahead.

2. **Schedule some downtime.** Many of us with chaotic, hectic lives forget to plan quality time for ourselves and our friends and families. Yet that's exactly what we need every week to feel rejuvenated and peaceful within ourselves again. Also, having something fun to look forward to with those that you love (human or animal) has this surprise benefit: Studies show that merely anticipating a vacation or weekend away actually boosts happiness. You don't have to take a vacation, though, to feel the positive effects of downtime.

Those that find it difficult to take time to relax and unplug actually need it the most, so try setting aside a few hours in the weekend to relax and have some fun. Your busy weeks will feel more peaceful knowing you have that to look forward to.

3. **Practice gratitude.** It's so easy to constantly compare yourself to others. They have it easier, the better house, more money and on and on. But learning to be grateful for what you *do* have (while remembering we all have struggles—even those who seem to have it so "easy" on the outside) can help you to put it all in perspective and bring more peace to your day. As Theodore Roosevelt said, "Comparison is the thief of joy"—and I certainly believe this to be true.

BEING PEACE WITH YOUR ANIMAL MEDITATION

Sit indoors or stand outside near your animal in a comfortable position, spine straight, shoulders and arms relaxed. Eyes remain open and in soft-focus. Place your hands over your lower belly. Relax your entire body as you breathe deeply a few times.

Imagine there are roots growing down from the base of your spine, deep and wide into the earth. Imagine that the powerful, grounding energy of the earth can flow up these roots into your lower belly giving you stability and peace.

Take 10 breaths, and on each inhale, feel peaceful earth energy coming up into your lower belly. On each exhale, release any emotions, fears or worries you may have out your roots, easily dissolving them into the peacefulness that is earth. The earth is so strong that it can easily dissipate these fears and worries into perfect pure light that nourishes. With each successive breath, feel more and more stillness and stability within you. Once you have completed the 10 breaths, allow yourself to relax in the space of earth energy and stability that you have created with your breath.

Once you feel yourself fully calm and connected to the earth, simply invite your animal into the peaceful space you have created with your breath. Imagine that within this space, all is perfect and balanced and that your animal can join you. Feel harmony enveloping both you and your animal. Let go of your expectations (along with any worries about what needs to be healed) and continue to breathe the calm and strength of earth energy into your belly as you share this space with your animal.

Place your hands gently on your animal if he approaches, or keep them on your belly if he chooses to remain at a distance. Signs of relaxation and stress-relief in your animal will indicate that he is sharing your peaceful healing space with you.

TRANSFORMATION 3: FEAR AND WORRY TO SURRENDER AND TRUST

Something amazing happens when we surrender and just love. We melt into another world, a realm of power already within us. The world changes when we change. The world softens when we soften. The world loves us when we choose to love the world. – Marianne Williamson

If we want to support healing transformations in our animals, we have to first visualize and embody the positive. So for example, if we're working with fearful animals, we have to focus on the opposite qualities of what they're displaying and work on holding those qualities within ourselves. And even more than just visualizing the quality, we must embody the quality.

Meditation can help us to embody positivity within our own being. So for example, rather than fighting against the fear, which actually focuses our energy towards the fear itself, we have to work to create a strong and clear energy inside of ourselves that's the exact opposite of it. In other words, we have to focus on creating and holding a foundation of calm, courage and trust. Meditation can help us to become a spiritual rock of solidity and dependability for our animals.

COURAGE MEDITATION FOR A FEARFUL ANIMAL

Sit indoors or stand outside near your animal in a comfortable position, spine straight, shoulders and arms relaxed. Eyes remain open and in soft-focus. Place your hands over your lower belly. Relax your entire body as you breathe deeply a few times.

Imagine there are roots growing down from the base of your spine, deep and wide into the earth. Imagine that the powerful, grounding energy of the earth can flow up these roots into your lower belly giving you stability and peace.

Take 10 breaths, and on each inhale, bring your awareness to the parts of your body that touch the earth. Imagine the earth is a giant magnet attaching you to her surface. Feel your body become heavy with the power of the earth magnet beneath you. Feel the earth's strength, solidity and power. Imagine the separation between you and the earth dissolves, and you become simply part of her ageless strength. Feel the power of the earth expanding up from her surface, into your body, filling your body with solidity and power.

When you feel yourself calm and connected, then imagine your heart can expand out of your body creating a beautiful state of courage and trust. To help you to do that, you can call upon memories or experiences in your life where you felt courageous or where you felt a deep, deep trust within your spirit.

Once you feel that sense of being courageous, invite the animal into that space and imagine that within that beautiful heart space, that space of courage, everything is in harmony, everything is in balance. You feel a strong bond of trust connecting you in the animal; make sure to let go of your expectations.

When working with fearful animals, it's very important let go of our own worries about what's going to happen, or what needs to be healed, how the animal is going to respond or what the outcome will be. We have to let go of everything and just breathe courage. Breathe calm. Breathe stability. Be that spiritual rock. Breathe it into your heart, and radiate it out for the animal to remember his own power.

TRANSFORMATION 4: FROM FIXING TO GRATITUDE

Connecting with animals within meditation is a way of connecting more deeply from your heart to the animal's heart, becoming more aware of the love and compassion that exists between you. Meditation reminds us of our deeper connection, beyond just the physical relationship. This heart connection transcends species and it even transcends life and death. Meditation helps us to be present from our heart. With meditation, an animal can be going through the dying process, and we can still support his journey in a very profound way.

When we meditate, we can relax our need to "fix" every situation, and instead begin to realize all the gifts the animal has given us through our time together. We can realize too that our animals are always connected to us in our hearts, so even though it's a very difficult journey, we can hold their paws through this dying process. There is nothing to fix, nothing to do. It is only a heart space of being present in gratitude.

I remember my meditation experience with Patty who was a German Shepherd mix who had been rescued by BrightHaven Sanctuary. She was in hospice, and I happened to be teaching a class that weekend. She wasn't doing that well that day, so I sat next to her to meditate and offer support. She looked up at me, and I just had a strong feeling that I should massage her forehead as I sat with her, which is really not something I would normally do, but I felt that she wanted me to do that.

Then I went inward to find the still point within myself. I felt meditation helping me to let go. I let go of worry about what might happen; I let go of trying to fix things. I realized that this was her final chapter in the journey. There was nothing left to do. The only thing I could do was to be with her. I felt myself putting each worry into a cloud and letting the cloud float away. I became calmer and calmer and more peaceful within myself. Within just a few minutes, she stretched her head out toward me. Her breathing became less labored. She became much calmer. Within a few more minutes, she had stopped panting. She sighed, and finally, I could see she was fully relaxing. What I felt personally in that moment when she really fully relaxed and we connected in that space, was this overwhelming emotion of gratitude and love surrounding us, flowing through us, between us, around us, and spreading out all around us.

I could feel how much she appreciated all the love and care she had received at BrightHaven; it was so touching and so amazing. I realized in that moment that this is what the dying process was about. It's about gratitude. But so many times, we still are in that mode of trying to fix and change or resist and so we miss it. Meditation helps us to just surrender, and when we do, we can really feel that love and gratitude so strongly. It is so beautiful.

She passed a few weeks later surrounded by everyone who loved her. She's still a part of my heart, and I'm so grateful for what she taught me about dying with grace and with gratitude.

BEING GRATITUDE MEDITATION

Sit or stand in a comfortable position, spine straight, with your shoulders and arms relaxed. Relax your entire body as you breathe deeply a few times.

Take 10 breaths, and on each in-breath, feel the earth energy coming up into your heart. On each out-breath, release any emotions, fears or worries you may feel inside you. With each successive breath, feel more and more stillness and stability within you. Once you have completed the 10 breaths, allow yourself to sit for several minutes in the space of earth energy and stability that you have created with your breath.

Once you feel yourself fully calm and connected to the earth, bring your animal to your mind. Allow yourself to think about the experiences you've had with your animal for which you are grateful. Focus on the parts of his or her unique being that are so special to you. Imagine that your heart can expand out of your body, creating a beautiful state of gratitude all around you. Thank you. Thank you. Simply invite your animal into the space. Imagine that within this heart space, all is perfect and balanced. Feel gratitude enveloping both you and your animal. Let go of your expectations (along with any worries about what needs to be healed) and continue to breathe the calm and strength of earth energy into your heart as you share this space of gratitude with your animal for as long as you like.

TRANSFORMATION 5:
FROM PITY AND SADNESS
TO COMPASSION AND
LOVE

True lasting healing is about peace of mind and heart, and this is what sharing meditation with our animals is all about.

I believe compassion to be one of the few things we can practice that will bring immediate and long-term happiness to our life. – Dalai Lama

Several years ago I worked with a shelter dog that had clearly been neglected in his past. His coat was very dull, his eyes stared blankly into space and he barked continuously. The shelter staff asked me to please try to help calm him because he had been hysterically barking since he had arrived.

So I sat quietly outside his kennel. I put in my earplugs and I took a deep breath, and I imagined the energy of the earth flowing up through my body, grounding and centering me, and I closed my eyes, and inside my mind, I imagined that I was in a quiet beautiful place. And then I added affirmations peace, safety, and harmony.

I held these three words in my heart and I imagined how the dog looked when he was calm and perfectly relaxed. I imagined I could embrace him with love from my heart. After just a few minutes, the dog stopped barking and stared intently at me. A few more minutes passed, and he lay down in the kennel, took a deep breath, and rested his head on his front paws.

How beautiful that silence felt. Meditating with this dog was a helpful tool for me to transform from a place of pity and sadness and go deeper into a place of compassion and love. We have to sit still and let our minds drop into our hearts. Only meditation can do that for us – especially if we are sitting with an animal that is suffering or unhappy. Meditation techniques help to bring us to a place of balance, calm, and a sense of deep connectedness. When we do this, we can get in touch with hope and open heartedness with others: people, animals and the world.

When our heart opens to another being, we feel an overwhelming sense of well-being and compassion. And it's this compassion that is the fruit of meditating with animals. To be able to sit with our animals who may be suffering, not in a place of pity and sadness, but rather from a place of deep peace and compassion, being truly present with them: this is the most profound kind of healing we can ever offer to others or ever experience ourselves.

RAINBOW HEART
CONNECTION MEDITATION

Sit quietly for several minutes and connect to the energy of your heart. Breathe in air from the earth into your heart. Visualize your heart as a beautiful center of white light within your being. Imagine this light is filled with all the love and compassion you have experienced in your lifetime. On your out breath, see this light, with all the colors of a rainbow, expanding from your heart, beyond your physical body, into your aura, the room, and out into the universe.

Next, bring to mind an animal in your life that you would like to connect with for healing in love and compassion. See the energy of the animal's heart as a beautiful center of white light within his or her being. Expand the rainbow of your heart in love, compassion, serenity, and peace to include the heart of your animal. Remembering that this light is merely an "offering" on your part, and that if the animal is willing your hearts can unify in a beautiful space of healing through this rainbow.

Spiritually, rainbows symbolize hope, harmony, and connection beyond the physical. Visualize your hearts unified in rainbow light and perfectly in balance, at peace, connected, and completely healed. Know that there is no situation that cannot be healed, that there is always hope, and that you will always be connected to each other, no matter what.

EXPAND YOUR STATE OF MIND TO HELP YOUR ANIMALS

Judge nothing, you will be happy. Forgive everything, you will be happier. Love everything, you will be happiest.– Sri Chinmoy

Through meditative techniques, we can learn how to connect with animals in profound ways. But sometimes our own humanness can get in the way of helping our animals.

When we are meditating with our animals, sometimes we can sense certain things in our hands or emotional feelings/intuitive information. It's very easy to find ourselves in a place of judgment and interpretation. However, the best way to help our animals is to let go of these impressions and open our minds to healing possibility.

My teacher Frans Stiene of the International House of Reiki teaches that in Japanese these impressions are called Hibiki—which means an echo. Thus, when we sense something from our animal, it is not a true experience, but rather our impression of the animal's true experience. This is a natural occurrence when we meditate, because meditation cultivates heart-to-heart connections. In this connected space, we often sense many things, but we must remember our impressions are always colored by our own filters.

When we experience these impressions while we are meditation, we have two choices:

1. We can focus on the impressions themselves and interpret them.

Or,

2. We can thank the animal for sharing with us (thus focusing on gratitude) and then let the impressions go.

The first choice will involve us focusing on things like "this or that is wrong" or "this is what needs to be fixed" and "this or that needs to be healed." Inadvertently, we end up focusing on the negatives of the situation. By doing so, our mental state becomes very narrowed and small. Animals feel this. I sometimes call this our "pointy" state of mind because we are unwittingly poking the animals with our negative thoughts. We can see this in their uncomfortable behavior with us, or they may say no to connecting with us.

Focusing on what's wrong can also give rise to pity. Pity can sneak into our minds when we are working with, for example, shelter animals that have come from a bad situation. They can feel this pity inside of us and it can also cause them to not want to connect with us.

The second choice creates a spacious mental attitude of gratitude. We can acknowledge and thank the animals for sharing with us, and then let the impressions go like clouds floating by in the sky. We want animals to feel our positivity, our openness, our light and our gentle way of being. Choosing this open and expansive state of mind will help attract animals (rather than repel them).

Letting go of judgments is also a way to see your animal as the empowered perfect being that he or she is, even in that difficult moment. In this way we are focusing on the positive. Think back on a difficult time in your life and remember how wonderful it felt for someone to hold positivity for you!

When we meditate with our animals, it's most important to stay in a place of openness and love in your heart and mind. Remember that all things are possible. The following quote is a great reminder when we feel discouraged:

You will face your greatest opposition when you are closest to your biggest miracle. – Shannon L. Alder

5 MINDFULNESS LESSONS FROM OUR ANIMALS

Sometimes when looking at my dog, I notice how mindfulness appears to come so naturally to her. She doesn't carry the weight of the world on her shoulders (okay, she's a dog–of course she doesn't!). But we can learn a thing or two from these mindfulness masters, our favorite cats and dogs.

Over the years, in my work with animals and also after spending so much time with my own animals, it has occurred to me that important examples in mindfulness exist right before my eyes, every single day. My animals live in this special mindful space we humans are always trying to reach (but rarely get there). It's so hard to "be mindful" when that same mind is filled with worries for the day, responsibilities for loved ones, tasks to accomplish and so on.

So whenever I start to feel overwhelmed (and therefore less mindful), I think about these lessons in mindfulness we can all learn from our animals:

1. **Embrace the moment right now.** When Mystic is sprawled in the sun for a nap or on a walk, she's not worrying about her next vet visit or wondering if another dog is going to turn the corner at any moment (these are two things she does not enjoy). Her mind is free and open to wander, since she's not stuck inside thoughts about yesterday or tomorrow. She's able to fully surrender to and enjoy each moment. Looking back on my life, when I'm able to really "be" in the moment, I feel so good. It's easier to be strong, centered and my true self when I remember to just "be." Though a to-do list often looms in my head, I try to remind myself that if I'm following Mystic's lead and losing track of time doing something fun, that means I'm doing it right!

2. **Don't just take your dog for a walk; embrace the walk the way your dog does.** Be curious and notice the small details and sights, sounds and smells, like: the sound of leaves crunching underfoot, the feeling of the sun on your

skin, the salty beach air and so on. When you focus on the beautiful world around you, there isn't as much room for worry or anxiety.

3. **Be silly and have fun!** Mystic doesn't always take herself so seriously. Sometimes, she's happy to play and romp around like a puppy. Just yesterday she was leaping like a gazelle through the tall grass on a hike. I swear she was smiling! We all can remember from childhood how good that can feel, and it's another way for us to connect with that mindful space.

4. **Do something new today.** Reliving routines over and over again allows our mind to slip into old patterns. We don't have to give our full attention because we've seen it or done it a million times before. The result? Our mind might wander to past or future worries instead of noticing the moment right now. But when we're doing a new activity, it forces us to focus on the moment at hand. For Mystic, this might mean chasing a lizard instead of a squirrel. For me, it could mean taking a new trail for our walk, using an alternate route on my drive or trying a new café instead of going to the same favorite places over and over again.

5. **Savor your favorite things; don't multitask.** This one can be especially difficult! But Mystic has it down pat. When she gets a new treat (peanut butter flavor is her favorite) or a few bites

of something I have baked (she loves muffins!), she's 100 percent there, savoring every last morsel. I guess when I eat chocolate: That's a time when I remember to savor.

3 REASONS ANIMALS MAKE THE BEST MEDITATION TEACHERS

Can I admit something to you? It isn't always easy for me to meditate. There are so many "human" challenges that can trip me up—an overactive mind that refuses to quiet, difficulty in accepting the present moment, or being so busy my energy is scattered all over the place. I want to share with you my secret weapon to strike down these obstacles and ensure a more powerful meditation: the animals.

Over the years I began to notice something interesting; when I would meditate and my animals would happen to be present, I found myself able to quiet my mind and be present with an open heart much more easily. I began to realize that perhaps I should rethink the way I approached my own meditation practice. Meditating alone is all well and good, offering numerous health benefits that have been backed by science. But when I began to meditate with the animals and follow their lead, all of the benefits of meditation I had always experienced began to improve. Here are three ways animals helped me become a better meditator:

1. It's easier to stay present and peaceful in the moment with our animals. If we are trying to meditate but our intellectual minds keep analyzing, judging and interpreting everything (which is just natural for us, really), the animals will often mirror this agitation. The more we feel ourselves shift into a state of quiet, and the more we can just "be," the more we can see the animals relax. I can always tell what state I am in by how the animals around me are responding to my presence. A peaceful mind and peaceful heart means peaceful animals. In addition, animals have a natural calming presence. So when we have trouble letting go, and we're stuck inside past problems or future fears, simply sitting with our animals can help to calm our energy, quiet our thoughts and take us to this moment right now.

2. Animals help our hearts to open, so that we can radiate our inner compassion. According to a 2013 study by Northeastern University, those who

practice mindfulness meditation feel more compassion for others. But sometimes, compassion can be a difficult feeling to tap into. That's where the animal factor comes in: Animals show so much unconditional love for us, we just can't help but open our hearts when we are with them. If we are with our animals during our meditation practice, our inner compassion arises effortlessly because we are already opening our hearts to our animals at that moment. This compassion will radiate out to all animals ... and even ultimately to the world.

3. Animals helped me realize an informal meditation can be just as effective. Some people think, "Oh, I have to light a candle and sit on this cushion to meditate." And that sometimes works well, but it's also very limiting. Meditation isn't about escaping the world, shutting our eyes and sitting in a stiff position. The most important purpose of meditation is to bring compassion to our lives, and the truth is we have to learn to take our practice off of the cushion, bringing this compassion with us into the world. What the animals teach us by their compassionate presence is very freeing: That truly any moment in our lives can be a meditation. We can practice peaceful presence while sitting, walking or standing— cuddling our cat, walking the dog or standing in a pasture with our horse. You see, this is how our animals live already, and they can show us how to live this way too.

Meditation is about bringing all of our energy here to this present moment, and opening our hearts to the peaceful power that exists in the now. Animals are always present, they don't judge like we do, and they live life with an open heart. They are my best meditation teachers: mirrors, reflecting to me how I should be, and lights, guiding me along the path of inner healing.

THE POWER OF ACCEPTING THINGS AS THEY ARE

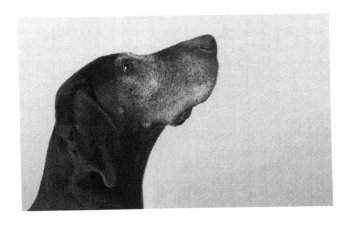

We all want to help our animals when they face tough times. But in order to do that, we have to be able to hold all things, good and bad, and to accept even the most difficult moments, rather than run from them. No one can live forever, and life always changes. All we have is this very moment. The more we can accept this reality and even embrace it, the more open our hearts become and the more we can support our animals when they face difficulties.

To accept things as they are, we must develop an inner spaciousness, where our hearts can open up. One way to do this is to reflect upon life's impermanence so we can embrace the moment. Here are three quotes to help you. Contemplate them in meditation or write about them in your journal:

1. *The butterfly counts not months but moments, and has time enough.* – Rabindranath Tagore

This quote inspires me to ask questions such as: What is time? Is it the past? Is it the present? Is it the future, or is it more?

2. *Bees have to move very fast to stay still.* – David Foster Wallace

What is movement and what is stillness? Can you experience stillness while you move? Can you experience movement while you are still?

3. *When you truly embrace your human impermanence, you connect with the power you have, and the influence you have, over the time you have.* – Steve Maraboli

What is true power? Power is often seen as something negative, but is this true power? Are you afraid of your own true power?

In one way, this present moment is illusory, as it always leads to the next moment, and the next and so on. And yet at the same time, there is so much depth to this present moment. There is so much love and goodness we can infuse into it. We must learn to see things with our hearts; in this way our fear of the impermanence of life loses its grip on us and we can live more fully in the present. For example, we might look at our animal who is ill or suffering and we can see the suffering with our eyes, but that is not all there is; it is only the surface of things. If we look deeper, with our hearts, we can also see our animal's inner spirit: a perfect, bright and beautiful light. No outward, changing circumstance will dampen this wonderful light. We can connect to this light each and every moment. We can share compassion and peace right now.

Accepting things as they are means that we can be present with the outer circumstances, which even when they are difficult, are always changing. At the same time we can bring our awareness to the deeper truth of the spirit, which is always balanced, bright and harmonious. Focusing on the heart of things will help us embrace impermanence, while offering unwavering, courageous support to our animals when they need us most.

WHAT HAPPENS WHEN WE HONOR FARM ANIMALS AS TEACHERS?

Those of us who love dogs and cats have experienced the many gifts to our lives they bring us. But what if farm animals, too, had many gifts to give, if only we would stop long enough to listen?

Have you ever gotten to know a pig, cow, chicken, sheep or goat? Chances are, your first introduction to some of these animal species was on your plate. We've built our human society around the idea that animals—in fact all parts of nature—are simply products to be used for human needs. It's because of this kind of egoistic thinking that our planet is in such a mess with global warming, destruction of rainforests, wars and so on.

But what would happen if we could find a way to open our hearts to others in compassion? If we could learn how to do this, everything could change and the world could heal. I think as animal lovers, a great and easy start would be to transform the way we view farm animals. What if we could open our eyes and see them for who they really are and learn from their wisdom?

Here are three spiritual lessons I have learned from farm animals:

The Cow: Forgiveness

When my daughter was a toddler, I'll never forget the day we visited a pumpkin patch before Halloween. A cow was living in a paddock on the property, and my daughter immediately ran to the fence. The cow walked over and stood with her head down just low enough so that my daughter could pet her through the fence. How touching it was to see the joy on my daughter's face and the recognition of this joy in the cow—how trusting and close she was with my daughter. As I wondered about this cow's future, I wished in my heart that this kind of sweet connection between children and cows could be repeated over and over in this world. No matter what has gone before in the realm of human/cow relations in this world, there is hope for change and there is space for forgiveness.

The Sheep: Gentleness

During one of my visits to Remus Memorial Horse Sanctuary in England, I had the good fortune to sit in meditation with the several of the sheep in their barn. They seemed fascinated with my practice and had all gathered near the fence, watching me as I sat and breathed peacefully. After several minutes, one of the older sheep came slowly out of the barn. Clearly, she had some difficulty walking and was very unbalanced on her feet. As she came forward to the fence to see me, all of the other sheep parted quietly and gently like the sea so that she could walk unimpeded through them to greet me. She moved so slowly, yet the other sheep happily gave her whatever time and space she needed to move freely. It was so beautiful to watch how they respected her and showed this with such gentleness. I thought to myself, if only humans could treat their elders in such a manner, society would be very different.

The Chicken: Focus

I love visiting the chickens who live in the garden at my daughter's school. Have you ever watched a chicken hunting for seeds, leaves, bugs—well, just about anything to eat? They are so focused that nothing gets past them. They can find the smallest seed, unearth the most hidden insect and gulp down a piece of lettuce faster than the human eye can follow! And as long as any seeds remain, they will keep working for them through scratching and pecking. It is so sweet to watch, and I think to myself, if only I could be as focused!

In this day and age, we have become so distracted by so many gadgets and technology. We are always doing several things at once, and I think this takes away from our experience in the moment. Perhaps we can follow the examples of the cow, sheep and chicken and turn our focus toward finding ways to honor others and transform this world through compassionate action. I hope so.

BONUS MEDITATION FOR ANIMALS AND PEOPLE IN CRISIS

Many of us feel helpless when there is a disaster and animals are involved. Being so far away from the disaster, it's easy to feel helpless during tragic times like these. But there are things we can do, however small.

Making a donation to a charity is one way to help. Another way that I've chosen to help is to offer this special meditation of peace and healing for the animals (and their people) affected by a disaster. Meditation is always something I can grab onto, no matter how down I feel. I hope it helps you, too.

HEALING MEDITATION FOR ANIMALS IN CRISIS

Find a comfortable place to sit, with your beloved animal at your side if you wish. Place your hands, palms together, in front of your heart, and dedicate this practice to all the animals and their people affected by this disaster. Then rest your hands on your lap or on your animal. If your animal is close to you, he/she may want to support you in this meditation.

Close your eyes as you breathe. As you inhale, imagine the breath as a beautiful healing light flowing up from the earth and through your body to your heart. On the exhale, imagine your heart as a bright light that expands to fill your whole being and then out into the universe. Inhale strength from the earth into your heart; exhale the bright light of your heart into the universe.

Continue this breath at your own pace for 10 repetitions. Then allow your breath to return to normal and breathe gently.

Turn your mind toward the animals and people in need. Feel the light at your heart shining so brightly. Repeat in your mind,

> May you be free of suffering.
> May your heart feel peaceful.
> May you be healed.
> Know that you are loved.

Continue to repeat these words in your mind for several minutes as you feel them radiating out.

Imagine the light of your heart shines so brightly that it can reach all animals and people in need. Your light is so bright that any darkness or suffering disappears. If you feel distracting thoughts, imagine they are clouds just floating by. Don't chase them; let them come, and let them go.

When you are ready, set your intention to finish, take a nice, deep breath and slowly open your eyes.

Know that even simple acts of heartfelt compassion ripple out into the universe in powerful ways.

JUMP START YOUR MEDITATION PRACTICE WITH THE 5-3-1 HAPPINESS CHALLENGE

If you're not in the habit of meditating here is my challenge to you. Practice the following three actions every day for the next 21 days and see how your life has transformed.

1. Mediate using one of the meditations from this book for five minutes a day: Remember, your daily meditation doesn't have to take place sitting in a quiet room on a pillow with your legs crossed. Meditation is about bringing compassion to our lives—and then sharing it with the world. You can do this while walking the dog, taking a stroll on the

beach, cuddling your cat and so on. These forms of meditation may be considered "informal," but they're just as powerful—if not more so. I also prefer to meditate with animals close by. Since all we need is five minutes a day for this challenge, try the meditations in this book as a launching point.

2. Write down three things that you're grateful for in a gratitude journal: I'm grateful for my health, yes, and for my family, etc., etc. But also challenge yourself to look deeper and uncover new things specific to each day to be thankful for, the little things that pass by and get forgotten because so often, life just moves too fast. So instead of "I'm grateful for my daughter," look for more focused gratitudes, such as, "I'm grateful that my daughter and I were able to share some laughs during breakfast this morning."

3. Practice one random act of kindness: Be a little creative about it. Think about sending a little thank-you note or email to someone who helped you recently; you could also purchase the Starbucks latte for the person behind you in line at the drive-through. You can also look for opportunities throughout the day that will arise for you to do a conscious act of kindness on the spot.

FINAL THOUGHTS

A human being is a part of the whole called by us universe, a part limited in time and space. He experiences himself, his thoughts and feelings as something separated from the rest, a kind of optical delusion of his consciousness. This delusion is a kind of prison for us, restricting us to our personal desires and to affection for a few persons nearest to us. Our tasks must be to free ourselves from this prison by widening our circle of compassion to embrace all living creatures and the whole of nature in its beauty.– Albert Einstein

When we want to help animals find peace through mediation, we need to remember that we're part of something bigger. All of the transformations I have shared in this book are in reality about transcending our humanness and meeting the animal in a deeper space of heart, of spirit, and of soul. This is a place beyond species, beyond illness, beyond sadness, beyond aggression, beyond fear. Meditation can bring us to this transcended state where peace and compassion can create miracles of healing. Compassion is the center of the universe and the center of our hearts.

When you open up to the ultimate, immediately it pours into you. You are no longer an ordinary human being. You have transcended. Your insight

has become the insight of the whole existence. Now, you are no longer separate. You have found your roots. – Rajneesh

IF YOU LIKED THIS BOOK,
TAKE THE COURSE!

This book is based on a course called "5 Powerful Meditations to Help Heal Your Animals," which members of the Shelter Animal Reiki Association (SARA) teach in a variety of locations. In order to experience a deeper understanding of the teachings in this book, SARA President Kathleen Prasad recommends that readers take an in-person course with a SARA teacher or SARA practitioner in their local area.

For more information on attending the next session of "5 Powerful Meditations to Help Heal Your Animals," please visit:

www.ShelterAnimalReikiAssociation.org.

ABOUT SHELTER ANIMAL REIKI ASSOCIATION (SARA)

SARA's founding principles are:

Passion - Commitment - Service

The mission of the Shelter Animal Reiki Association (SARA) is to improve the lives of animals by promoting the use of meditation in animal shelters, sanctuaries and rescues worldwide through education, training, specialized research and the advancement of meditation programs that meet the highest standards of integrity and professionalism.

SARA is a 501(c)3 nonprofit that supports:
- health and wellness of animals in shelters, sanctuaries and rescues.
- caregivers at each animal organization.

Through meditation and Reiki training programs, SARA educates:
- interested shelter, sanctuary and rescue staff and caregivers.
- interested veterinarians.
- animal lovers in the community at large.

SARA seeks to promote Reiki's standing in the scientific community by:

- supporting ethical and animal-friendly animal Reiki research studies.
- creating alliances with the veterinary community.

Through SARA's ongoing professional development, training and evaluation program for members, SARA seeks to:

- promote the highest standards in Animal Reiki Practitioner and Teacher excellence.
- provide ongoing support for Animal Reiki Practitioners and Teachers volunteering in shelters, sanctuaries and rescues.

If each of us does his or her small part for the animals in our lives, imagine how those little acts of compassion can build up and grow all around the world. – Kathleen Prasad, *Reiki for Dogs*

Kathleen Prasad and Leah D'Ambrosio founded SARA in 2008. SARA is dedicated to the memory of Dakota, Kathleen Prasad's beloved dog and the inspiration for Kathleen's work in the field of animal Reiki.

For more information, merchandise and to make a tax-deductible donation, please visit SARA's website at

www.ShelterAnimalReikiAssociation.org.

ABOUT THE AUTHOR

Kathleen Prasad is founder of Animal Reiki Source and president of the 501(c)3 nonprofit Shelter Animal Reiki Association (SARA). She has taught Reiki meditative wellness techniques to thousands of animal lovers around the world, as well as the staff and volunteers of organizations such as BrightHaven, The CARE Foundation, Remus Memorial Horse Sanctuary, Best Friends Animal Society, The San Francisco SPCA and Guide Dogs for the Blind.

Kathleen has authored the books *Reiki for Dogs, Everything Animal Reiki, How to Help Animals With Reiki* and *5 Powerful Meditations to Help Heal Your Animals* and co-authored the books: *The Animal Reiki Handbook* and *Animal Reiki: Using Energy to Heal the Animals in Your Life.* She's been published in magazines such as The Journal of the American Holistic Veterinary Medical

Association, Animal Wellness Magazine, Animal Fair, Equine Wellness Magazine, The Whole Dog Journal, Dog Fancy, Feline Wellness and Dogs Naturally Magazine, and featured in several radio and TV programs. Considered the world expert in this field, as well as a dynamic speaker and passionate advocate for spiritual wellness of animals and their people, she has been invited to England, France and Australia to teach and speak about Reiki for Animals. Kathleen offers courses around the country as well as regular classes at BrightHaven Holistic Animal Retreat in Santa Rosa. She also teaches a variety of correspondence and tele-classes.

62109861R00043

Made in the USA
Lexington, KY
29 March 2017